FUN-SCHOOLING
FOR MOMS
OF PRESCHOOLERS

How to Help 2, 3, and 4 Year Olds Learn

While Having Fun at Home

Georgia Janisse & Sarah Janisse Brown

THE THINKING TREE

PUBLISHING COMPANY, LLC

"We hope and pray that book inspires you to create a delightful environment for learning with your little ones!"

www.2-isms.com

Table of Contents

1.

Fun-Schooling With Preschoolers

Most of what two, three, and four year olds learn, is learned through exploration, experimentation, investigation and imitation – they actually teach themselves. Playing is their job and their schoolwork. And just like explorers discovering, scientists experimenting, athletes using their skills, and artists absorbed in creating – they love their job! Your main job as their most important teacher is 1) be a good model to copy, 2) provide safe opportunities for your little ones to teach themselves, and 3) answer their questions.

Preschoolers learn through play. As they are having fun with cars, dolls, legos, games, swing sets, mud pies, play dough, listening to you read, coloring, sweeping the floor, dancing, asking question after question, singing, looking at books . . . whatever interests them, whatever they want to play with, they are learning.

Many of the strategies in this book can begin to be used in the toddler phase too - starting when the little ones are able to understand and follow simple direction. The first chapter is about the uniqueness of two year olds: how they think and what motivates them. In Chapter Two are suggestions about teaching three year olds and easing them into this (potentially) delightful transition year. And the chapter on four year olds explains how to make use of their natural their curiosity, creativity, and confidence to direct their learning with amazing results! The rest of the book is practical how-to instruction for working with your child's nature to help them learn both life skills and give them a foundation for academic education - all by fun-schooling.

You can read straight through this book, but it's okay to just read the chapter describing the learning needs of preschoolers by age level, and Chapter Four: "How to Communicate with a Preschooler." It is about Language – one of the most important things that we learn from other people. After reading these chapters, you can skip around the book to learn about what you want to, or need to.

2.

Understanding Two Year Olds

Little babies are little bundles of potential, but so helpless. The amount of knowledge that must be learned just to get by in this world is so immense, it's impossible for us to grasp. For example: as adults we know all about the objects we see; just by looking, we can tell that an object is soft, rough, or smooth, but we learned to recognize these textures by experience. Luckily, we don't have to figure out how to teach these things to children. They seem to pick up this kind of knowledge automatically, but in reality they must teach it to themselves. So, all that touching of things they shouldn't and playing with things that aren't toys . . . is really their personal study program.

As soon as babies move from the womb into our world, their drive to learn is working (once they can get past the surprise of their whole new world, of course). It's fascinating to watch babies for signs of concentrated interest. How precious it is to hold a baby in the first moments of life and make eye contact – you will see the look. It's a look of deep concentration, fascination, and focus. You can almost see the little wheels spinning in their heads. This instinct to learn tends to rule their interests until they are about three years old. They have a LOT to learn!

New babies have very little control over their learning opportunities. We need to be aware that babies are really at our mercy when it comes to mental stimulation. It isn't until they learn to move their bodies that they can reach out, pick up, then crawl over to objects in their world. A toddler is a baby that can walk. A toddler's greatest delight is practicing all those new skills like walking and climbing to explore his world – especially if it's baby-safe. This phase can be tiring for parents. But life with a toddler is still mostly fun, and you can understand them – because you realize that they are still just babies.

Then, somewhere around their second birthday, your child is able to walk and run without thinking about how to run. Now the focus of interest shifts. They want to know everything about anything in their world. They become little scientists who must test the properties of the objects they find interesting. How does it feel, how heavy, how hard, what sound does it make if you hit it on the ground? What happens when you throw it, kick it, stomp on it, wash it, or flush it? You can still see the look of concentration, if you watch for it. They will try some of their experiments over and over. It is at this point (when a child has learned to control moving without having to pay attention to moving), where I feel that the stage they call the "terrible twos" begins.

To enjoy two year olds, there are two things you need to know:

What Motivates Two Year Olds,

and How They Think.

It is amazing that children will pick up the language and culture where they live, while learning all about the unique part of the world they live in. If a newborn African baby girl was adopted by Austrians, she would grow up speaking German and have no idea how to carry water jugs on her head. Human beings have some truly instinctive behavior – those things that are the same for all people all over the world like the facial expressions that show happiness, sadness, surprise, anger, fear, and disgust. But most of what we do is not instinctive, we must learn how to do the things we do – and that is how it is that the amazing variety of lifestyles, cultures, and languages are possible.

I can't emphasize enough the incredible amount of things each of us needs to know, and so many of these things must be learned between the ages of two and three — so these little ones come equipped with a drive to learn. Their drive to learn is as real a drive as hunger or thirst. We understand many of our children's needs: food, shelter, a place to sleep, diaper changes, hugs, love, and so many other things necessary to their health and well being — and we provide them. But during and in between all those needs, is their need to learn. Their play is their work; it's how they learn. A child's compulsion to learn is essential for his survival.

Two year olds are motivated
by the need to learn.

How they think

If you have a two year old in your life, then you already know that they don't think the way we do. So, how do they think? Well, the main issue is how they don't think - they don't think verbally.

Most of us begin to think in words around age three. True, they are talking now – using new words every day! But they don't have a large enough vocabulary or grasp of how words work together to think in words. (I'm not sure how a person can think without words. Are their thoughts mostly pictures and feelings?) So when you say "What is he thinking!?" you are asking a very good question.

A two year old might be able to say a lot of words and understand even more, and yet not understand sentences. I know a lot of Spanish words, but I am not fluent – and I certainly can't think in Spanish. When I spent two weeks in Nicaragua, a woman that I had been getting to know walked up to me after a meeting and told me something in a sentence ending with the words "no es muy bueno" and obviously wanted a response. Knowing I had to say something, and recognizing immediately the words "muy bueno" (very good), I responded "gracias" (thank you). As she walked off in a huff, I went through her words in my mind – I had recognized all of them but her sentence was just a little too long for me to understand instantly. I had to translate the words one by one into English before I realized, too late, what she was telling me: something I was personally in favor of was, in her opinion, "NOT very good." (I suppose that my odd response was probably about the best answer I could have come up with if I had known what she was saying!) Two year olds - no matter what language they are learning - speak it as a second language, and have to translate the words into whatever form their thoughts take.

Understanding that two's are not verbal thinkers helps your enjoyment of them in two main ways:

1. not making assumptions about their motives
2. communicating with them

Assumptions

With thoughts in forms such as pictures, touch, movement, sounds, and emotion you can imagine that decision making must take a very different path for them than it does for us! When anyone makes assumptions about the motives of a two-year-old, their guess may be WAY off. We make assumptions about their motives when we think "He knows I don't want him to do that, so he is doing that to defy me" or "To do what she just did, I would have to be really angry, depressed, afraid, hateful, wanting control, revengeful, or uncaring. . ." You might imagine the same emotions that drive your actions are motivating your child, but consider this: even when you try to put yourself in your child's place by remembering what it's like to be a child, it's unlikely that your thinking can go back far enough, because nonverbal thinking is the main reason very few people can remember anything about their life before age three.

Communication

Knowing how to speak in a way that your child can understand will save so much frustration for both of you! Wise parents know it is vital to spend time chatting with, explaining things to, and reading to your little one. In fact there is probably nothing more important that you can do for your child's mental development.

But when you have something very important to communicate:

1) Speak slowly and clearly
2) Use simple words they know
3) Keep your sentences very short - two to four words
4) Repeat
5) Repeat using different words.

There is a lot more about this subject in Chapter 4 – How to Communicate with a Preschooler.

3.

Three Year Olds

Somewhere around their third birthday, children begin a major transition in the way they think! At this age, about ninety percent of people begin thinking with words. But remember that not all children are growing up in the same ways at the same time. For example, the 10% who become visual thinkers will develop powerful memories, amazing creativity, the ability to view and imagine things in three dimensions, and to think in ways that enable them to "see the big picture;" But at three years of age these imaginative children can be impulsive and seem more like two year olds in the way they make decisions. So remember that each child is unique; intellectual and personality traits that seem like a problem in early childhood might just be great blessings in adulthood. Enjoy them as they are. Don't focus on how they compare to other children their age.

Three year olds are entering into a delightful stage of life! It seems like all the boys are superheroes and the girls are princesses. Make sure you have costumes for them! Imagining themselves as a hero, as someone important, is something we want to encourage. Think back to what you wanted to do and to be when you were a child – eight or ten or twelve. Even now, thinking about the fun and the excitement of actually living those dreams, should bring a smile to your face - whether you actually accomplished them or not! At three you can be anyone you imagine! And you can be something different on different days! How wonderful is that!

If you have older children, your two, three, or four year old will want to be like the big kids. They want to do what the big kids do. And they will want to do what you do. Put this trait to good use! See Chapter 6 for specific ideas.

A child who is two years old usually enjoys being around other children, but their play is more side-by-side play than really playing interactively together. Three year olds start building friendships! They are now learning to play games and make-believe together, to have adventures, and to work together – but the children will need lots of direction as they first begin learning to play together. Always be where you can see and/or hear as they play. Give just enough fun ideas to get them started, and be ready to help them learn how to work through squabbles in a calm and friendly way. With young threes, step in at the first sign of disagreement. In families there are often children of different ages playing together. Don't make the mistake of always making the older child give in – three year olds are ready to learn how to share and to treat others with kindness.

Playing games is a wonderful way to learn so many helpful skills and good manners. When it's a fun game we naturally want to know the rules. Some of the valuable skills learned by playing games are: learning and following practical rules, taking turns, meaningful counting, following directions, and getting used to the idea that sometimes you lose! Just try to be sure that the game is not too hard for the child, or it will become frustrating. But they can join in a game that might be too advanced if you can play as a team: "It's our turn now. Don't knock over the playing pieces when you roll the dice!" "Pick up one of the yellow cards and let me read it."

One of the best, most fun – and sometimes exasperating – traits of three year olds is all their questions! They have now entered the age of "Why," which usually doesn't reach its peak until about five. So learn to enjoy it. The investigative reporters and inductive Bible study teachers could have gotten their training from watching these little ones asking "who, what, when, where, why!" Take the time to answer their questions. At the moment they ask a question, their mind is open and tuned in for learning! Take these teaching opportunities seriously and be ready to give – or help them find - the answer. How wonderful if you have a book on the subject and can show pictures and read aloud to them about it. Never discourage your child from asking questions, even though sometimes you have to let them know that it's not the right time to ask. There is more about questions in the next chapter. Encourage their inquisitive minds! And if you do want to teach them about something, find a way to place the question in their minds first.

A special warning about teaching children to count: preschoolers need to know, right from the start that numbers represent a quantity. Don't teach them to just memorize saying "one, two, three, four . . ." as just a series of words, without relating it to real amounts. Count real items with them. Try to make counting multisensory – not just visual, use touch and movement and sometimes even sound. For example: How many blue cars do you have, hand them to him one by one and count until he is holding all four; then go over to the toy box and count again as he drops the cars one at a time into the toy box.

Often three year olds are expected to be learning the names and even sounds of letters, and how to count and recognize numbers. If your child is curious and asks to learn about letters and number – then teach then. Answer their questions. But if they are not interested, don't worry. It is amazing how fast a child can learn a subject when they are developmentally ready to learn it. They will quickly catch up with kids who have been drilled for years.

4.

Four Year Olds

The three words that best describe four year olds are: curious, creative, and confident.

Curious

People just naturally love a mystery and puzzles. If we hear the beginning of a story we will want to hear the end too. A good teacher will find a way to put a question in the mind of the students before teaching about a subject, because, when we want to know, we will listen, we will try to understand, and we will remember. With four year olds there is no need to create a lesson plan that is designed to catch their attention with a mystery or a puzzle to figure out. They will take care of that part for you. Here is the secret: all you have to do to teach four year olds is to ANSWER THEIR QUESTIONS.

The thrill of mystery; the concentration needed to solve a puzzle; and the curiosity to know how the story turns out - are all wrapped up in those questions! Every time you answer his question, your child will learn with interest and remember the lesson well. If a teacher can get the class to laugh, or feel shock, heartbreak, or joy: they will not forget the lesson. Because, when emotion is connected to a memory, it becomes easy to remember. The child who asks a question is already feeling curious, is delighted that you will answer, and finds excitement in learning the information. So, answer their questions. If the child asks a question at a time when you are unable to answer immediately, tell them you will think about how to answer, and help them keep the question in their heads by suggesting that they draw a picture of what they are asking about (a planet, animal, clouds, blue sky . . .) Then get back to them as soon as you can (don't make them wait more than half an hour).

If you are not sure about the answer you can look it up together. Maybe you have a book on the subject. You can check the internet. Years ago we would have a set of encyclopedias ~ ha ha. If you have been happily answering lots of questions and there is a question that you really don't know about, you could suggest that they ask someone who does know. Maybe an aunt, uncle, or grandparent happens to know all about horses, airplanes, the solar system - and loves talking about it! You could give them a call or suggest that your child asks when he see them (if you expect to see them soon). Or tell your little one that you will get books about it on this week's trip to the library. Maybe you should even write down the question, so you won't forget.

If you have older children and your four year old starts asking questions about a subject one of the big kids is studying, let them look at their textbooks. If a four year old shows intense curiosity, you could even have the older child give lessons to the little one a couple days a week - as long as they keep showing interest. There is no better way to learn than to teach, so they will both benefit.

What you just read is based on the way my daughter homeschools her four year olds. Here is a list of questions — written down word for word one day when one of her sons was four years old. And this is only 40 minutes' worth of questions!

1. How fast does Jupiter spin.
2. How fast do electrons orbit around the nucleus of an atom?
3. How fast do the bones inside the ear vibrate?
4. How long does it take to get from our house to the beach?
5. How far away is the moon?
6. How long does it take to build a house?
7. What kind of atoms make rocks?
8. What kind of Atoms make orange juice?
9. How far away is London from our house?
10. What is the biggest number on money?
11. Can people make money that is the same amount as Pi?
12. How do electrons make electricity?
13. What kind of atom has the most electrons?
14. How fast does the earth spin?
15. Did you know that the femur is the biggest bone in your body?
16. Did you know that the smallest bone is in the ear?
17. What is that bone called?
18. What gases are in Saturn?
19. What is water made of?
20. What exactly is H2O - what kind of Atoms are they?
21. What happens when animals die?

You can see that a child has to have a lot of knowledge, understanding, and curiosity to ask questions like this!

Three to five year olds can exhaust their busy parents with questions. It's so common for adults to discourage them from asking questions. That is so sad! Encourage your child's curiosity and love of learning. Choose to be delighted by each question. Even if you have to tell them that you can't answer right, at least tell them that it's a great question or that you are happy that they asked. Never say the words which have been said by millions of parents: "Stop asking so many questions." Let your child feel comfortable bringing every question to you.

Curiosity is the key to real learning. Remember, Albert Einstein said, "I have no special talents, I am only passionately curious."

CREATIVE

At four years old a child can develop the skills needed to really show their creativity! Teach them how to use scissors, glue, tape, watercolors, poster paints, paint brushes, stamping with rubber stamps, sponge or potato stamps. Let them try play dough, and craft clay that can be dried in the oven. Mix up recipes together to make play dough (flour, salt, salad oil, and water), silly putty (white glue, with a few drops of a solution of borax in water), foam paint (shaving cream, with a few drops of white glue and food color). You can get exact recipes on line or in craft books. And let them use their imagination.

It's great to teach them to make simple crafts that they can use as ideas for their own unique creations later. I love to find ways to use their drawings to make something special. Teach them to make and decorate paper frames. Cut out the pictures and use them as part of another craft idea – a greeting card, or to decorate a folder. You and your children can make up your own crafts. If you do go to the internet to find a craft idea, I suggest that you keep in mind just finding something that you have the materials for and that will easy to show them how to do, then stop searching and just DO IT! Don't keep looking for the very BEST craft. My husband needs to keep telling me that "perfection is the enemy of getting it done." Even an ordinary and very common craft is new and exciting to the child who is doing it for the first time. If you try to get dozens of ideas you will probably forget most of them and not be able to find them again anyway – and you just spent an hour online rather than with your child. If you get a craft idea book from the library, buy one, or have one on your shelf - just open it up and do one. After that it will be easy to do more.

But there are so many other areas of creativity: music, dance, singing, drumming, cooking, storytelling, playing games! Inspire creativity by making up new games, or a new twist on old games; costumes and make believe; making little dolls and jewelry from flowers and leaves; designing forts and tents and finding dozens of uses for cardboard boxes! See the Chapter 10, Learning Activities: Having Fun with Preschoolers. Give four year olds some ideas and some supplies and then let them do it their own way.

CONFIDENT

They are excited to learn, but want learn about the things they are interested in and curious about, and they are also interested in everything that other people in the family are interested in. They see themselves as SO BIG. They want to be just like mom, just like dad, like the big kids, a princess or a super hero. They love to work alongside parents, and if trained can be very valuable helpers.

Some of the common problems seen in four year olds are - whining, copying the bad habits and attitudes of other family members (and characters in videos they watch), and easily get sucked into spending tons of time on video games and movies. But the reality is, four year olds would much rather spend time with family. They would rather talk with people. You can ask your little ones questions! They love to talk about what they like to do, and about subjects they have been interested in and learning about!

Curious, creative, and confident. These are strengths that you want to encourage and keep strong. So be sure to let them know when they are doing something good, working hard, or being helpful. We must correct bad behavior, but be sure to tell them what TO DO. Not just what NOT to do. Train them to do the things they are trying to do to help you. They can learn to do chores that are too hard for three year olds. Keep them moving forward in their skills and jobs. But always remember how young they really are and know that they will need encouragement and direction all through most of their tasks - even though they can do much the work themselves.

I always like to encourage children's accomplishments and their hard work: whether it is a household chore, a creative activity, learning new knowledge - and I tell them things like — "Wow, I can see that you really worked hard on this!" "Doesn't it feel good when you know you did such a good job!" "I love the way you even wiped off the counter after washing all those spoons and bowls!" When you feel appreciated, you do more. I think too many people see work as unpleasant, and entertainment as good. Do you want them to have a happier and more productive life? Keep teaching them to enjoy helping others, have a good attitude toward work, and to appreciate the wonderful feeling completing a job well done.

5.

How to Communicate with a Preschooler

After reading my book on two year olds, Matt (not his real name) may have been thinking: "It can't be this easy. If these things really worked wouldn't everyone be doing it, and two year olds wouldn't act the way they do?!" One of my daughters had given him an advance copy of this book; being the father of a two year old, he immediately read it cover to cover. The next day, as he buckled his little daughter into her car seat, he failed to notice that he had left his map book on the back seat. As he began to drive he heard the sound of ripping paper.

"Sweetie, don't tear Daddy's book." (Hmmm, no, he couldn't reach her while driving.)

No reaction, just the sound of paper calmly, slowly being torn.

"Daddy needs that book. Don't tear Daddy's book." (Spoken with a little more authority in his voice.)

She ignored him and kept up her slow destruction of the book.

Then my words flashed into his mind – "Don't tell them what NOT to do. Tell them what TO do."

"See the pictures.   See the pictures in the book?   Look at the pictures. Look at the pictures in the book."

The ripping stopped.   Matt's little two-year-old daughter was looking at the pictures, and slowly turning the pages.

How is this possible? How did that work? Why did it make such a difference?   What could possibly be going on inside that cute little head? Is it possible that we have misjudged and misunderstood two year olds? People ask: "Why does my two year old do the opposite of what I say, and then throw a temper tantrum when I get upset about it?" It can be frustrating to be the parent of a two year old, but imagine how frustrating it must be to BE two. We know that they understand a lot of words, so we assume that they understand us when we talk. But two year olds do not think the way we do. We don't realize how abstract words like "no" and "don't" are. Twos have a very hard time trying to visualize or grasp negative words.

If you have ever tried to learn a foreign language, you are familiar with the process. You can study books, take classes, learn on the computer, even listen to it spoken and practice saying the words, but you can only go so far without spending time talking with people who speak it as their first language. When you start interacting, you listen to hear words you know and try to figure out what is being said, then search your mind for the right word to say. If the person you are talking with speaks too long or too fast you lose track of what is being said.

In applying this to a little child consider a sentence like "we are going into the library now so don't make a lot of noise and don't run." What would be the one word he'd remember first – you got it: "RUN." And he didn't hear the word "NO" at all (it was hidden in the word "don't"). My friend in Nicaragua (Chapter 2) had no idea that I wasn't following her sentence, because we'd spoken enough that she knew I understood a lot of words. But apparently she hadn't taken note of how often I said "repito por favor" and "mas despasio" ("please repeat" and "more slowly," the most used phrases of those of us who don't yet think in the foreign language yet we are really trying to understand).

So we need to use two totally different ways of talking with a small child, in two different types of situations.

normal speech for everyday conversations

simple, clear speech for important information

How to Chit-chat with Preschoolers

First let's look at normal everyday chit-chat. It feeds their drive to learn. Among the things a child is learning and developing as we talk with them are:

- language and how to talk
- a meaningful relationship with us
- how to interact with people
- knowledge about their world
- getting their brains ready for more complex thought.

In the book "The Mislabeled Child" parents are encouraged to "make sure your home is a rich and nurturing language environment" in order to prevent and to treat a variety of learning disorders involving language.[3]

Some examples of everyday speech and conversation are:

- listening to and answering their questions
- reading to them
- telling them stories
- teaching them poems and nursery rhymes
- telling them the names of things
- asking them questions

Most of the time we don't think about how we speak. But even in everyday conversation it is a good idea to think about it once in a while. So often when we speak, all the sounds that make up the words zip past the ears of small children so quickly that they have trouble separating the words within the sentence and telling similar sounding words apart. When you slow down and pronounce words very clearly as you discuss whatever the child is showing an interest in, he will listen to you, because you are making it easy for him to make sense of language.[4]

One wonderful way to enjoy little ones is to give them words and opportunities to use them. Most children hear a lot from television, but have little real back and forth conversation. Take the time to listen to them. Talk with two to four year olds about the things they are already interested in. Speak in complete sentences, with a full vocabulary of names of things, of action, and description. You shouldn't use baby-talk yourself, but you don't really need to correct theirs. Listen patiently, and give them time to find the words themselves. When your child asks you a question, you have a wonderful teaching opportunity. With younger children, answer their questions simply; with older children you can go into more detail – just watch for signs of boredom! Then you can have a conversation about the subject. With older threes and four year olds sometimes you can ask them questions that will help them to figure out the answers for themselves.

Ask them questions about things they have recently done or seen. Talk about some of the important things that can't be perceived with their senses, like our emotions: how helping, and hugs, and enjoying being together are ways of showing love, etc. Read to them, tell them nursery rhymes, teach them songs, and be willing to read the same book or the same poem, over and over. The fact that they are enjoying the repetition means it's fulfilling a learning need. One of the many benefits of reading to your child is that they get to hear the same exact words many times, giving them a chance to figure out the exact sounds of the words and meaning of the sentences. Another reason to read to children is that the books will have words you don't often use, and often sentences put together in ways that are a little different, enriching their language. Asking about the pictures and characters can sometimes start wonderful little conversations.

How to Communicate the Big Stuff

The second kind of talking with a preschooler, is talking to communicate important information.   There are times when it is essential that the child understand you. In order to keep them safe you must make warnings very clear.   Other examples are when correcting their behavior, when teaching them a simple skill, or when they are having a tantrum. Here is what you need to know in order to successfully tell them what they need to know:

When it is very important that they understand you

- Speak in very short sentences – two to five or six words at most (more with a calm older child – fewer with excited or younger children).
- Use simple words – if possible, ones you've heard the child use.
- Speak slowly and clearly.
- Repeat exactly what you said, and also repeat using different words.
- Tell him what to do, not just what not to do.
- Make sure you have the little one's full attention. If possible talk to children before they get excited and distracted.
- Keep the total conversation short.
- Ask the child to repeat what you said. You may need to help with this.
- Tell Them What TO Do, Not Just What Not to Do

A negative sentence can be very confusing to a little one, so think of a way to put the information in the positive. For example,

Rather than saying:	Say:
"Don't be so loud."	"Speak softly," or "Be quiet."
"Don't go in the street."	"Stay on the grass," or "Walk on the sidewalk."
"Don't pick the flowers."	"Just look at the flowers. Smell the flowers."

When you need to use a negative word or phrase, do it in a very clear way – contractions can make the sentence difficult for a two year old to follow.

My granddaughter Marian had been visiting me one day when she was two years old. As she and her mom were leaving, Marian spotted my big bright orange daylilies and ran over to pick one to take home – I stayed right at her side. Before she could touch them I engaged her in talking about the flowers (twos love to get the words to go with things they are interested in) "These big flowers are pretty!" "Do they have a smell?" We checked for fragrance and talked about the color. She reached out to pick it and I said (sadly) "No, no picking the big flowers. No picking grandma's big flowers. See these little flowers? You can pick them!" I showed her my honeysuckle vine. "Mmm, they smell so good." And I helped her pick some.

By the way, if you look you will find that almost any lawn has some little flowers growing in it – searching for them and picking them is a fun activity you can do with little ones. Even little clover leafs can be fun to collect. Help them find something fun that is okay to do.

Think of situations you have encountered in the past and try to imagine ways to give directions that are positive, short, and simple. They really need to know what they CAN do - not just what they are NOT allowed to do. After all, it might be easy to use words to talk about not doing something, but it's really hard to visualize or feel something that doesn't happen. Preschoolers tend to be "concrete thinkers" – they think in terms of things they can see, touch and feel. Give them words that their little not-yet-verbal, or concrete thinking brains can use!

In the next chapter I'll talk about heading off tantrums before they start. But the reality of it is that – especially with two year olds - tantrums can't be completely avoided. If your child is having a meltdown and you communicate with him in this way, it will not stop the behavior instantly. But it can help to begin the calming down process. Keep your communication as short as it can possibly be. Start by letting the little one know that you understand the source of his frustration, tell him what he cannot and can do, then ignore the awful behavior. This should shorten the whole process. The downside is that anyone watching will think you are crazy and ineffective – but you'll know the difference. The self-confidence and calm you project will surely impress any onlookers, including your spouse! If you can't control the child, at least you can control yourself.

6.

Helping Them to Be Good

My daughter Heather is the mother of four boys and was running a licensed home day care. When I asked for her view of twos and their frustrations she wrote:

"I think people forget to baby two year olds because of all the changes that come with being Two. No more bottles/nursing, no more crib, no more being spoon fed, a lot less being carried around... on top of that two year olds WANT to do everything themselves. They want to open and close all the doors, throw away the diaper, hold the toothbrush (theirs and mom's), carry heavy things, and basically take over or imitate any task that mom or dad is doing. The combination of those two things seem to make adults forget that just months before they were thinking of and treating the two year old completely different. Adults try to anticipate a baby's hunger and sleep needs, and they hold, cuddle, talk to and "help" babies all day long. I notice a lot of parents trying to make the two year old communicate those needs all the time, instead of anticipating them, and just freely giving drinks, food, and down time."

She summed up the predicament that two-year-olds find themselves in:

"Babies have all their needs anticipated and met - preschoolers can communicate clearly and in an acceptable manner - but poor two year olds aren't having all needs anticipated, and also can't communicate effectively."

In other words, we bring a lot of unneeded frustration into the life of the child. They can do so much. So, outwardly we see them as capable, but inwardly they are still in many ways babylike. Just as teens in the transition from childhood to adulthood are not really adults or children, the two-year-old stage is the transition from baby to child. Maybe this has something to do with why parents generally find these two stages to be the most challenging.

Parents know that preschoolers really do need lots of guidance from adults. Children need loving parents to be in charge – set limits, make rules, and enforce them. But that does not mean there must be a battle for control! In fact, I believe that when parents see their job in raising and caring for a two to four year old as a battle for control, then their approach will actually become self-fulfilling: if the parents and caregivers continually stand in the way of a child's built in curiosity and opportunities to learn, with a "I tell you what to do, you don't tell me what you are going to do" approach, then that necessary learning drive will force him to fight for every possible learning opportunity he can get. Or even more sadly, sometimes a little one may just give up and begin to lose the love of learning. It may be that imposing this battle for control upon your relationship can drive a wedge between parent and child that sets the tone for life.

On the other hand, when we love someone, we listen, we pay attention, we are concerned about them, and we want to meet their needs. We build a bond of trust as we recognize that the little one is simply following an intense and indispensable drive to learn. We lay a foundation for future learning. Sometimes it is necessary to say, then enforcing, "no," but the best kind of correction is to first try turning the child's attention away from dangerous or challenging behavior into a more appropriate activity. Raising a well behaved child is a good thing, and so is raising a happy child – a confident child who gets along with others, loves learning, and reaches his potential.

Don't say "NO" unless you mean it!

I know - you want me to tell you how to control the child. But, I know preschoolers, and especially with two year olds I try not to expect more than they can deliver. I've seen parents whose thinking process seems to go something like this: "Okay! She can walk and talk – now I can treat her like a seven year old. I'll tell her what to do and make her obey." That's just not realistic. Obviously, there are times when the child must obey. So, I'll get right to the point. If you tell a child to do something, or not to do something – in the form of a direct command - be prepared to make it happen.

On a visit to my home, my grandson, Joseph, was playing with the buttons on the T.V. I told him to stop, but he didn't stop immediately, so I got up and moved him away from it if. It took a couple tries before we were able to get him interested in something else. It would be foolish to punish a two-year-old for this type of infraction.

Punishing a child for acting his age usually has unintended consequences, like:

- They learn to ignore the punishment because it becomes such a regular part of daily life.
- They may become confused, not connecting their action with your re-action.
- Constantly stopped from showing curiosity, they can lose their love of learning.
- You can lose your ability to be consistent.

Years before many of us knew anything about brain development, I would tell other parents to "just keep getting up and making them obey. Be consistent, and eventually they will figure out that if you say something, they will end up doing it, and they'll realize that they may as well obey on their own" and I always added: "they'll figure it out about the time they turn three." It is also clear that if you aren't consistent when they are two, they still won't do what you ask when they are three (or four, or five . . .). By age three to three and a half, usually children will be more socially focused and they will understand the pattern of your discipline. Consistency is just as important for older preschoolers, maybe even more important.

If you say "no" more often than it is truly necessary then all this consistency can get real old real quick. You don't want to ever give up and just let the child do what you told him not to.

PICK YOUR BATTLES CAREFULLY

- Before you give an order, ask yourself: "Am I willing to do whatever it takes to make sure this happens?"
- Have as few "no's" as possible.
- Ask yourself "what's it gonna hurt?" when deciding whether to create or remove rules.
- Focus on the serious issues.

Obviously it's hard to be consistent when you have lots of rules and lots of no's. On the subject of making rules for your kids, my husband says: "decide which mountain you want to die on" (he's also a retired US Air Force Chief Master Sergeant). In other words, just as a company of soldiers shouldn't try to defend, or to take, territory unless they are ready to fight for to the end; you shouldn't command a child to do something that you aren't willing to carry through with - no matter how much the child tries to resist. (Yes, this is a pretty radical example, but I really want to get through to you on this issue!) Oh, and the "pick your battles carefully" was one of my husband's sayings too.

We all know that being consistent, following through, and doing what you say are basics of child training, but too many rules or no-no's make following through every time into an unrealistic goal.

When you keep it simple,
being consistent becomes possible.

Giving commands and getting obedience

Often we need to get a child to stop what he is doing, put down what he's holding, change his behavior, or you are going someplace where certain behavior is required (quiet, walking only, keeping hands in pockets, holding your hand . . .) These are basic skills needed for guiding and directing preschoolers:

1. Make sure they understand – keep your words clear and simple
2. Prepare children for change – the two minute warning
3. Redirection – help them move on to a different activity
4. Show them how to behave – be an example to follow
5. Breathe deeply and slowly, stay calm (I'm serious)

I'm a real believer in taking the time and trouble to PREVENT discipline problems. Do these things and you will be working with your child's nature, and not against it.

1. Make sure they understand:
keep your words clear and simple

After you have done your best to tell them clearly what to do, ask them to tell you what you just said. With two year olds this is especially important: "What will you do when I talk to the lady?" –"Sit. Read book." If your child can't tell you what you said – just do what language learners always ask for: repeat and speak more slowly. And once again, be sure to tell them what TO DO - rather than what NOT to do.

2. Prepare children for change: the two-minute warning

Actually, it's more of a five minute warning: "We are going to leave soon. You can play five more minutes," followed in about five minutes by "We are leaving soon. Please help me pick up the toys – you can be my helper!" Better yet, give them something to help you carry out to the car. All too often, change surprises little children. They aren't expecting it, and they have trouble adjusting, so give them a little warning – four or five minutes is enough. If it doesn't work the first few times you try it, keep it up anyway – it may take time and experience for them to really see how it works (and how long minutes are). This little warning can save you from so many temper tantrums! And it is helpful with seven year olds and seventeen year olds too.

Charity's daughter Mimi was two years old, and had been playing in her wading pool long enough. But for Mimi it was never long enough! So Charity was not looking forward to the battle to get her out. She was one of the first to read this book and decided to try one of my suggestions by preparing Mimi for change with a five minute warning, and redirecting her with another activity. She announced that in five minutes it would be time to get out of the pool and get dressed to go in the car to Grandma's house. She asked her twelve year old to stay and watch Mimi for a few minutes while she got her purse. Returning to the backyard ready for the fight, she found Mimi out of the pool and towel dry, smiling and ready to get changed for the outing.

3. Redirection:
help them move on to a different activity

One big key is to give them an alternate activity. When the child is doing something that (how can I put this) is a bad idea, begin by considering what it is that has captivated his interest, then:

- think of something that might fulfill the same learning need,
- suggest it as though it is the most fun thing ever, and
- show them how it's done.

Heather was at an outdoor party with other young families. A little two-year-old boy had spotted the pebbles covering the pathway and garden border and was tossing them on to the grass. His mother kept pleading with him to stop, as she explained the damage rocks can cause to lawn mowers, but he kept tossing rocks into the lawn. So Heather got down on his level and formed a little pile of rocks in the path, saying "let's make some mountains!" He joined in and after a minute she went back to her conversation with the boy's mom, as he happily and harmlessly made little pebble hills.

When you give a preschooler an alternate activity, then the child must choose to either fight you and stubbornly keep doing what he's doing, or give in to your suggestion. So be a person they can trust for fun. Like them, we also listen more carefully to some people than to others. If we think of someone as having good ideas, we will be more interested in what they have to say. To enjoy a preschooler, it's good to be a person they look to for help in following their drive to learn. It often helps if the activity is related to the one they are doing – it is much easier to make a small change in their behavior by giving them something to do that helps them satisfy their curiosity.

4. Show them how to behave: be an example to follow

The next chapter is all about how and why preschoolers copy other people, and the amazing power of example. Notice how in the example above, Heather started doing what she wanted the little boy to do. Demonstrating exactly what you are asking them to do is such a great aid for the pre-verbal thinking style of twos, and is helpful for people of all ages!

5. Breathe slowly and deeply. Stay calm.

Be calm and confident. Confidence gives you an air of authority, and brings you respect.

Do Yourself a Favor - Simplify

Simplify your home a little. You can cut out so much stress and so many no's at home by putting easily damaged precious items out of reach, and better yet – out of sight.

Also, remember that those dangerous chemicals and sharp objects that you put out of reach when your little one was crawling and toddling around the house, may now be accessible to a resourceful preschooler. Try to think and see your home through the eyes of a child who wants to see, touch, test, and generally play with everything possible. Get on your hands and knees and take a tour. Then do a little rearranging. Home should be a safe refuge for us all – with as few temptations, dangers, and conflicts as we can make it.

And then, when you are on the way to the house of someone with lots of breakable knickknacks, talk to them about the special way they must ask before touching anything there - and maybe give them a special little stuffed animal or other toy to hold, to help them keep their hands occupied in an acceptable way. It can be amazing how well a little one understands that you need to act differently in different place, IF you explain it to them clearly just before they get there.

Why you may need to tell them
ALMOST the same thing over and over

Two year olds, especially, can't generalize well. In other words, if a situation is not EXACTLY the same, they may not see it as being the same at all. Perhaps you taught your daughter not to walk too close to your swing set when another child is swinging and you see her always watching – then you go to the park and she walks right in front of the swing. It is a totally different swing set. To us it is obvious. To a two year old it may not occur to them that it is even similar. In the same way they may not realize that sharing their truck or crayons follows the same rules as sharing their candy or dinosaurs. Try to imagine how the world might look with their limitations, and be ready to carefully explain almost the same thing again and again.

Heather has said of each of her boys when they were two and three: "It's a good thing he's so cute!" I believe there is an important reason why preschool age children are so cute – so we'd naturally have tender and merciful hearts toward them. Sometimes you just can't help smiling at the crazy things they do. In fact, there are times when I am with one of my daughters that we have to avoid looking at each other, in order to keep from bursting out laughing at the hilarious antics of her naughty little one. A tender heart and a sense of humor really help make it possible to enjoy preschoolers!

7.

Preschoolers Watch Us,

Then Copy Us

All day long we are using a powerful tool: EXAMPLE. Unfortunately we often use it mindlessly, enabling our little children to train themselves to do totally useless behaviors. Speaker and author, Gayle Erwin, is a dear friend. He tells about standing with his thumbs in his

belt loops. He didn't even realize that he did that, until he noticed his little son studying him then carefully placing his thumbs into his own belt loops.

To put the power of example to work for you, I want you to ask yourself two questions:

1. How can I model things I want my child to do?
2. What naughty things might they have learned by watching?

How can you model the things you want them to do?

Think specifically. Imagine real actions you can do to model the behavior you want to see.

We have an amazing gift for training preschoolers: they automatically copy us. They carefully study us and teach themselves to do amazing things that we could never teach them if we tried. Just watch the video on my website: 2-isms.com of the little boy playing his toy guitar next to his father. Could you imagine trying to teach a two year old how to act like a real guitar player by just telling him exactly how to hold the guitar, and describing in words strumming with a 'lost in the music' expression while swaying to the beat, but from time to time get a more serious look and adjust the knobs or keys . . ?

Once when my daughter Sarah was visiting my house, her phone rang. When she realized her phone had disappeared, she looked at Joseph (the little guitar player in the video) – in fact her husband and all the other kids also looked at Joseph. Sarah took the phone from him, read the message, and pressed buttons (while dodging Joseph's attempts to get it back). She gave the phone to Josh (the big guitar player). He texted an answer - while holding it over his head.

"He won't leave the cell phones alone!" they complained.

I asked Josh & Sarah "Do you know why he is so interested in it?" "Uh, because it lights up and makes sounds?" they guessed.

"No."

" . . . It has buttons that really do things?"

"That helps, but it's not the main reason."

They stared at me and thought for a while.

"Because WE play with it?"

I smiled and nodded.

I didn't think they were convinced, so I spotted among the toys in my living room, one of the most visually boring items: a little bean bag my mother had made years ago. After I silently demonstrated examining it and squishing it, I tossed it to Sarah - who had just put the cell phone out of reach and out of sight, so Joseph still had his eyes on her. She played with it a little, doing a good job of looking totally fascinated, then she and Josh started tossing it back and forth. They ignored Joseph until he tried to get it, so they included him in the game of toss, until he walked away with it - studying it and feeling the little beans inside.

The brains of young children are designed to pay attention to what we do, and then give it a try. Think about it - they truly NEED to learn what people do with the things in their world - it's a huge part of their built-in drive to learn. They watch us, and then copy us. And they don't just watch us. I've been paying attention, and I'm convinced it's the main reason for that exasperating preschooler behavior of: seeing another child playing with a toy then trying to take it. They obviously are not learning from their actions, since so often the result is crying, fighting, and getting scolded. Is he thinking: "I know there are lots of toys here, but I want to be mean and take a toy someone else has"? I think they are not thinking at all, just doing what they are driven to do - copy the people around them. (To know how to teach kindness, it helps to understand what motivates them.) I have found that if there are two preschoolers and you have two identical toys, they will happily play with one each – at the same time, side by side.

Heather, my daughter with the licensed home daycare, had purchased a cute child-size play kitchen. She showed it to the kids, but they ignored it. After a few days she had a flash. She just went over to it and pretended to cook at the stove, using the little pans, utensils and plastic & wooden foods. Without a word from her, kids came over to play and it soon became one of their favorite play areas.

So what are your goals? What do you want them to do that they aren't doing? How can you demonstrate, rather than only describe? Possible areas to consider using the power of example are:

- reading
- eating healthy foods
- turning off the TV when the show you wanted to see is over
- sharing with others
- dancing and singing
- saying "please" and "thank you"
- using the toilet (generally: father/son, Mother/daughter, son)
- washing your hands
- doing chores with a happy attitude
- saying "yes" to requests
- hanging the towel back up
- putting dirty clothes in the hamper
- enjoying the outdoors
- being kind to animals

You need to give thought to your goals for your child. Many of these things you already do all the time, and just need to make a point of letting your child see you do it. And one word about reading, if you do all your reading on your cell phone, or other electronic devise, your child may think you are just checking Facebook, watching a video, or playing a game. I believe that it's a good idea to let them see you reading print books. For those who want to encourage love and respect for the Bible, you may want to consider using an actual Bible. Seeing you read holding a real book can create a powerful image in your child's memory.

What naughty things might they have learned by watching?

This second question probably requires some soul searching. You might have remembered seeing someone else, like an older child, set a bad example that started an undesirable pattern. It's hard to control the example others are setting, but maybe you can take this information and gently explain it to whomever it is who might be creating a problem. Now, the only person whose actions you or I can actually control is ourselves, so it's important to think about the things we are doing, but it's so hard (and sometimes quite painful) to look at ourselves objectively. *Sometimes what we are doing is obvious to everyone but ourselves.* And yet this is where you really have power to change your little one. Try, as I have already suggested, staying very calm and speaking in a soft voice when your two year old throws a temper tantrum, and see if the fit is shorter than usual. If, like most people, you have been getting frustrated and showing it, then you might feel foolish if you don't react – after all this is serious; you should be upset! But stay cool anyway. Even if it doesn't help the child, it's great to have someone around who is calm when others panic – and it feels really powerful to be in control of yourself.

This is so important, in issues large and small. They *will* copy us. We need to be aware. Gayle Erwin also says "My wife and I worked really hard to teach our children good table manners, but it didn't work. They eat like me." Next time your child is doing something annoying, ask yourself – "Am I looking into a mirror, and seeing what my actions look like to others?" Don't be afraid. Take a very honest look at yourself. Self-knowledge is like the shot of Novocain before the doctor or dentist gets to work: sure it hurts, but it saves you from a lot more pain than it causes! So be honest with yourself and let your child teach you. Your little one might just be doing you a really big favor - by helping you become much more self-aware and a better person.

Controlling the examples in your child's life may mean that you restrict who your little one spends time with. You will also need to supervise closely, talk to family members, and choose babysitters carefully. Even pay attention to characters on TV, and videos. It's so important to be open to changing some of the things you do and say. Maybe you will realize that you are doing that same thing that one of your parents always did and you said you'd never do! Here is a list of some of the problem areas that might spring from example:

- poor manners
- getting angry often or easily
- sloppiness
- impatience
- negativism
- ignoring others
- too much screen time
- laziness

- poor grammar
- using crude language (or worse)
- lying
- destructive behavior
- talking back and arguing
- poor eating habits
- teasing

Maybe it's just me, but seeing people argue with children is one thing that just drives me crazy. Not so much children arguing with each other — that's a natural activity that can help them learn how to work things out. I'm talking about adults and children arguing with each other. We've all seen preschoolers who argue with their parents (and we all know that it takes at least two people to have an argument). I like the way my daughter Heather handles arguments with kids. She decides before she says "no" that it is something she will not change her mind about – wisely, she normally says yes unless there is a very clear reason to say no (not leaving herself any room to give in to argument). She is now able to stop her older boys quickly by saying "When Mom says 'no' does she ever change it to a 'yes'?" You have to have history backing you up for that to work!

"NO!"

Another common problem in preschoolers is negativity. Especially for many two year olds it seems that their favorite word is "NO!" But since I have been researching and studying two year olds, my daughters have really made a point of making sure that my two-year-old grandkids have lots of yeses in their lives, and not too many no's. In focusing on their brain development - by allowing the natural learning drive to guide their child's activities, rather than focusing primarily on behavior training - it turns out that their behavior is being beautifully shaped by their love of copying us.

To explain what I mean, here is an example from something my daughter Sarah did. A couple months before this writing Sarah decided to spend a few days saying "yes" to every reasonable request her children made (she was homeschooling her eight children ages thirteen to two).

Sarah wrote on a Facebook post:

> "For the past three days I didn't tell my kids what to do. I tried to say "YES" to ALL their ideas and requests. I made an effort to supply them with whatever supplies they needed for any project. Then I followed them around and took pictures. They kept

quite busy... And they only asked for my help a few times."

Looking at the pictures she took that day I can just imagine:
"Mommy, can I color with markers?" - "Yes!"
"Can we play Monopoly?" – "Yes!"
"Can I look at your coins from other countries?"
"Can we mix baking soda and vinegar and watch it fizz?"
"Can I bake a cake and make it look like a castle?"
"Yes, yes and yes!"

She kind of ended up with a habit of just saying "yes" to her kids a lot. Her two-year-old son got used to hearing Mom say "yes" immediately after he asked for something (anything reasonable, of course), and he began copying her by quickly saying "yes" and then doing what he is asked. Who would have thought?!

Not always, but often, habits, good and bad, get started by following someone's example. It is sad to think that a child is making himself and others miserable by doing what comes naturally: copying other people. A two or three year old just doesn't have the ability to reason why something is okay for someone else to do, but wrong for him. How good it is when this natural ability results in a more charming and happier child. The power of example is not a magic wand, but sometimes it seems like it!

8.

Making Chores Fun

It's so wonderful that *two and three year olds have a natural desire to help out.* Instead of plopping your youngster in front of a TV, computer, phone or other screen so you can get your housework done, enlist him as your helper. I know. I know. I know. It is SO much easier to do the work yourself. But what about when your child is seven, and is a willing, skilled, and experienced helper? – all because you took the trouble to train him when he naturally wanted to help. Of course, this book isn't about surviving and enjoying life now, it's about helping your children learn, and about making a better future.

This book is about understanding the natural motivations of two, three, and four year olds, and working with their nature to help them learn and develop life skills. Their desire to help out can be a wonderful asset – it has little to do with getting the chore done, and everything to do with your child's development, learning, and happiness.

You are the parent and also their primary teacher all the time. Don't try to divide your life into categories: this is when I clean the house, this is when I exercise, this is when I do yard work, when I cook, this is when I homeschool the older kids, when I go shopping, when I have quality time with my offspring. . . Your little one shouldn't be an item on your to-do list. Find ways to safely include your preschooler into as many daily activities as possible.

There are so many wonderful benefits of letting your child help with chores. Your little helper will:

- have fun
- learn practical skills
- learn to enjoy the satisfying feeling of completing a "job well done"
- practice following a series of steps
- feel that he has a valuable purpose in life (I'm not kidding – this is basic to happiness for anyone)
- spend meaningful quality time with you
- keep alive his love of helping others
- be closely supervised while you work (which could save you a lot of time later when you clean all your cosmetics out of the bedroom carpet – cartoons on the IPad can't always be counted on to captivate.)

HOW you recruit their help is important

Don't just say "Clear off the table," say "Help me clear the table." And it's not "Go get the broom" it's "I'm going to sweep the floor. Come and help me." "You can be my helper" and "I need your help" are exciting phrases to preschoolers. Before you call them, have a plan. Know what part you want them to do.

Show them what to do and work together.

Tell them each step of the job, in simple words and short sentences, one step at a time. This is especially important with new tasks. And give them feedback. Tell them when they are doing well, and help when they start to slip up. Have fun. Let them see everyday activities as something to enjoy, and let them know you enjoy doing things with them.

More than once I've been visiting a friend or relative and have seen the two year old run excitedly to get the little child-size broom the moment mommy starts to sweep. And mom always looked so proud! Working together doesn't necessarily mean that the child has to do real work. In the days when most clothes would wrinkle (except for polyester leisure suits), I had a friend who gave her daughter a toy ironing board set. They would do their ironing together. The little girl would "iron" her doll clothes and they would chat like grownup ladies. It was so cute. She said she had fond memories of "ironing" beside her mother. Personally, I usually found ways to avoid ironing altogether.

Here are a few ideas for ways your little one can be a helper:

- Put something in the trash for you.
- Bring you something.
- Help set and clear the table.
- Put clothes in the hamper and hang up towels after a bath.
- Wipe up spills.
- At stores, put items into the cart & take them out at check out.
- Help water plants (outdoors, unless you want to risk root-rot from stealth overwatering).
- Help feed animals.
- Take scraps out to the chicken coop or the compost pile.
- Help stir pancake or muffin batter.
- Press pause on the DVD.
- Pick strawberries or tomatoes.
- Put flowers in a vase.
- Wipe off a table.
- Hold the dust pan for you.
- Help carry things in from the car especially "big" or "heavy" things.

Just remember, with a preschooler, you are working together. You might be able to hand a stack of napkins to your five year old and find one next to each plate at the table, but with a two or three year old - I wouldn't count on it. You might just find them used as teddy bear blankets or clogging the toilet. Give the napkins to your little one when you take out the plates and silverware - and supervise. *Pushing a child into any activity they aren't ready for usually takes the fun out of it; and the last thing you need to add to your little one's life is extra* stress and frustration! Keep chores as a fun activity that he will look forward to.

You may even want to phrase the call to help as an optional request "Would you like to help Mommy?" This way there will be no argument. It's the child's own choice to make, so it is a win/win situation: they say "yes" and you get to spend quality time together in a practical educational activity, or they say "no" and you can get the chore done without all the hassle of their help.

9.

What to Do About Tantrums

Temper tantrums, meltdowns, and conniption fits, whatever you call it – this is the point when your adorable little sweetie "has lost it." Screaming, crying, throwing themselves on to the ground, clenched fists, and kicking feet are pretty standard. But some children have their own personal tantrum style. From our perspective it can feel like an attempt to hold us hostage to their will: "Do what I want or you know what will happen!" But in the case of two year olds, the child is experiencing an overload of frustration. The reality is clear – the child is not only out of control: he's lost control. How can we control them if they can't control themselves?

Three and four year olds who throw tantrums may also have a problem with frustration, but are also likely to be angry, or trying to manipulate you. In this section I'm focusing primarily on two year olds. Many of the strategies will be helpful with older children too.

My approach to discipline is to focus on *preventing* bad behavior. So this chapter is not exactly a plan for dealing with problems. But since bad behavior will happen, this chapter has some basic principles, and a few specific tips — what you can do during a tantrum. I have found that most people have pretty strong feelings about child discipline and will do what they feel is best for their family. I've already talked about staying calm, so I hope I don't have to remind you not to let anger drive your responses to your little one.

Avoiding Temper Tantrums

The best way to handle a tantrum is to avoid it all together. Think back to what triggered meltdowns in the past, and plan to prevent the frustration that so easily overwhelms twos. By the time a child is three, their temper tantrums are often learned behavior for dealing with problems, like not getting what they want, and these suggestions will help with that too.

We already talked about smoothly changing activities. For some children, stopping them in the middle of their play can be traumatic.

> As an artist, I know the frustration of being "in the zone" working on a painting — and being interrupted. I've learned to be polite about it. But sometimes the flow is lost and I have a sense that the painting that was developing will never be quite what it could have been. It seems that it feels the same way for a small child in the moment of being told to stop now.

Two year olds take their work (which is of course what their play really is) just as seriously! We need to help them with the change. Give them a warning — a little time to finish what they are doing and mentally prepare to do something else. If the "something else" is something they don't want to do — a more fun little activity in between might ease the change. Some activities naturally come to an end by themselves, like carrying something big or heavy back to the car (house, bedroom . . .), racing or marching to get there, getting a drink of water, or being your helper. So when this new task is complete you won't need to deal with ending the fun once again!

Another major tantrum trigger begins when your child asks for something that you do not want him to have. This is not an issue like making them eat what you serve for dinner; it is something that you can actually control. They are at your mercy and they know it.

It is a big mistake to ignore their request, or even to just say "no." If you do that, children will usually try harder to convince you how much they want it, how important it is to them, what a great idea it is. Their frustration level rises because they are sure that if you just listened and understood you would get it for them or let them do it. But if you keep ignoring, saying no, and telling a child why you won't buy the item/allow the activity, without first acknowledging their point of view, there will often be a meltdown.

We all have seen older children do this as a ploy to get what they want, but, as I said, tantrums in a two (especially a young two) are usually caused by overwhelming frustration. So, take action before anyone is upset.

Right at The Beginning

In the Early Whining Stage:

1. Listen to the request.
2. Tell them you know they really, really want it.
3. Confidently (not with irritation – sound like you really care) say "no."
4. If they still argue, do step 2 & 3 again.
5. If you want to give a reason for your denial, keep it simple, short, and honest. (Note: saying "I can't afford it" makes no sense to a preschooler.)

Try this and you will be amazed by how much the child wants to know that you listen and you care – maybe even more than he wants the thing that was so important. This pattern of responding actually even works with teenagers and just about anyone else too!

Responding to Tantrums

But what about those times when you are not able to prevent a tantrum? It will happen. In the chapter on communication I talked about how to speak to a child having a meltdown. The simple, clear communication will not stop the tantrum — but it will help begin the calm-down process. Your goal should be to help the child become calm — without doing something that will encourage future temper tantrums. Don't give them what they are crying for. If it is something that you want to give them, it's best to wait until the child is calm. Usually the real cause is an overload of frustration, and your goal is to help your little one learn to handle frustration, and become more patient. Demonstrate calmness. And, there is nothing wrong with completely ignoring them while they melt down, as long as you stay close by.

Press their Reset Button

In the height of a meltdown, a two year old might not be able to really hear or see or understand anything. But there comes a point where the child is able to take in a little input from you. Now is the time to "press their re-set button." When you have your hair dryer on high for too long, it gets overheated, and it turns itself off, then you have to let it cool down for a while and then you must press the little red button in – the reset button - before you can turn it back on. When the little one is beginning to calm, sometimes they get stuck in just crying or repeating some action or words – try a total change of subject, attitude, and action: "Oh my goodness!! I totally forgot that I wanted to check and see if there were any roly-poly bugs under the rocks in the backyard!" Use your imagination.

Correction

The most difficult area of discipline is when correction is required. Issues like: hurting another child, and putting himself in danger – after being told specifically not to. Stern disapproval and a no-nonsense time out, are the common first options, but always look for a way to "make the punishment fit the crime." Examples are: clean up the mess; the toy is put up; the activity is ended; if he hurts another child, it's time to stop playing together. Make sure you clearly and simply explain the connection between the act and the punishment, whatever form of correction you use.

Remember the goal of discipline is to change

future behavior.

I also feel strongly that one of the most important things you can teach a child is honesty, so, if the child told me what really happened, and the only way I knew about a bad action was the child's confession - I won't give the child a harsh punishment. If a punishment "fits the crime" the child will usually see it as fair, and be more apt to learn from the experience.

Each child is unique. Some are naturally compliant, but it is possible that most of the more typical two year olds – stubborn, self-willed, and noncompliant – have such an intense drive to learn that it is very hard for them to see a greater value in obeying you, anyone, or anything else. You've probably heard the commercial tag line: "Obey your thirst." Well, that's what the two year old does – obeys the thirst for learning.

Negativity

We all know that temper tantrums are much more likely when your child is hungry, thirsty, or sleepy. A child that is not allowed, or provided with, learning opportunities is hungry too – hungry to learn. It's sad, but it is common, for a two year old to get very negative: saying "no" to any suggestion, saying "no" to other kids, and just walking around saying "no" – over and over. So, as I already said, give your child as few no's as you can; really think about what your rules will be and make your home child-friendly.

Enable your little one to feed the need to discover, experience, and investigate. Learn to enjoy the noise children make when they are playing happily. Don't let yourself be irritated by their constant motion. Give them opportunities to "get their wiggles out." Spend time outside with them every day that the weather permits – and it doesn't have to be perfect weather. Or at least, put on some music and get them dancing. The very best discipline is preventative.

Creating new habits

It's important to be aware of how habits start. We don't want tantrums to become a bad habit, (the danger of giving in after the child cries long and hard) do we? Every behavior creates a pathway in the brain that makes it easier to do it again. It is a scientific fact that the more you do something, the more natural it is for you to do it again.[8] So by guiding your child into activities where he behaves well, you help him build habits of being pleasant to be around.

10.

Learning Activities: Having Fun with Preschoolers

Small children have a very short attention span – at least that's what we've heard. And when we try to hold their attention, we often find this to seem so true. And yet when they get involved in activities like the ones listed in this chapter, they are often able to focus intently for quite a while. Maybe what is called "attention span" is just the amount of time they are able to focus on what someone else wants them to do – rather than on what their inner drive to learn is telling them to focus on. Maybe the need to learn is so great that they naturally possess a very low tolerance for boredom. Their brain is telling them that what they are being asked to do is not something they need to learn right now – their learning drive is directing them to a different "educational opportunity" by telling them "Hey, it would be really fun to play with that thing over there instead!"

And so, for me one of the more frustrating things about preschool age children is never being sure that they will be interested in what I want them to do. I can have fun ideas, but the child is disinterested.

We cannot possibly design a curriculum to teach preschool age children all they need to learn, and there is no way to know exactly when they need to learn it. But the great thing is, their brain will provide the curriculum. Though they are not ready to learn how to read, write and work with numbers, they can play with letters, numbers, and learn by having fun with interesting educational items.

All we have to do is aid the child in their quest

for the actions, encounters, information, and

experiences that they are intuitively seeking.

Play Time Ideas

Alone or Together

Playing together is great and I talk about that in the next section, but it is also important for a child to have time to "work" undisturbed. We can give them some input to help them get started, then enjoy a break (kind of a break – you still need to keep your eye on them) as they:

- work on skills
- experiment to discover the properties of things in their world
- enjoy examining things
- investigate

Don't force undisturbed play; just make it an inviting option, in a quiet place where they won't be disturbed or too distracted. When they do focus all their attention on a task or examining something, they will get that expression of complete absorption (just like when they were babies). It's at times like this that their developing brains take the information they have been gathering and make new connections.

Here are some examples of activities that you can help your child be able to attend to without interruption. If you do them together just remember to not do too much of the work yourself.

Work on Skills:

- zipping, snapping, buttoning, using Velcro
- turning pages, opening and closing things
- eating a snack with a spoon or fork
- building with blocks, or other stacking toys
- dressing themselves, or their toy animals or dolls
- coloring, drawing, painting, paper tearing, pasting, play dough, mud pies
- balance and movement skills like hopping, jumping, climbing, dancing
- throwing, rolling, bouncing balls

These are the kinds of skills that, after a simple demonstration, the child can work on by himself. There is no series of steps or complex procedure to follow. For that kind of skill, the two of you need to work together. These are the kinds of skills that a person just has to get the feel for. As you supervise for the safety of the child, there is usually no need to interrupt their focus, but when you do give praise, encourage and praise their hard work and accomplishments.

Experiment and Discovery:

These experiments are ideal for solitary play and don't require much direction, though they generally require some supervision (the larger the amount of water, the more carefully you must pay attention to their safety). You provide the opportunity - all they have to do is play.

- pouring water from container to container
- making musical sounds – instruments for kids like xylophone, flute, harmonica, drum, guitar, tuning forks
- a pan, sink, or little tub of water and: floating items, funnel, sponge, soap . . . (don't leave them alone)
- sand, mulch, pebbles, gravel, snow, dirt, mud (you may draw the line where you wish)
- playing with shadows, a prism, flashlight

Your little scientist is very good at finding his own experiments too; if it is safe and harmless be sure to let him enjoy his research project. These activities can be done alone, while supervised for safety - both for the item and the child. They are wonderful things to do together too!

Examining and investigation:

- books, albums, catalogs
- plants, flowers, weeds, rocks, shells,
- pinecones, seedpod, acorns, leaves
- watching harmless insects like ladybugs, roly-poly bugs, and caterpillars

Toys

Some of the best toys have lots of different uses – like blocks or a wagon. They allow children to use their imagination. Some of the best toys don't cost much - like balls, little plastic farm or zoo animals, and toy cars. And at garage sales you can often find good quality toys which the youngest child in a family has outgrown. It's great to have a swing set or something to climb on, but nothing beats a sandbox!

Toys that challenge the mind and help a child be creative can be great for working together or for the child to do alone – if the toy is not beyond their abilities. Remember: learning what they need to learn now will be enjoyable for them. But if a creativity toy is difficult for your little one - work together on it. Examples of creative and learning toys are: puzzles, dress-up dolls, sticker books, coloring, play-dough, lacing cards, and painting.

Screen Time

TV, video games, and computers are to playing & learning, what candy is to eating. The kids love it and so we let them do it. But wise adults limit the amount. If kids are eating candy, then they won't have an appetite for more nutritious real food. In the same way, if kids are watching a video, they are not playing with real objects or with a real person. If you give the child a choice between a lollipop and an apple, they'll take the candy almost every time. And if a kid's show is on the TV, they'll usually watch it. [9]

Playing Together:

Expand their collection of ideas for play

It's great for you to do things together that will open the child's mind to new games, new ways to play, new areas to investigate or skills to work on. These are great ideas to suggest to babysitters and mothers helpers, too.

Make believe play

Make believe play can be based on real places they know about, like playing house, store, and restaurant; places and things they've never seen like a visit to Africa, Antarctica, space travel, and sailing on the ocean; or fantasy like being a magical princess or transforming into a robot. Remember games you liked to play, imagine new ones, or get an idea from the child, and run with it.

Sarah wanted her daughter Anna to keep the two youngest children in the family busy for a couple hours while she worked on a project in the kitchen. Since, like most eleven year olds, Anna often loses focus when watching her little brother and sister, Sarah knew that she needed more direction. I had given Sarah a printout of the chapter in my Two Year Old book (covering this information) to proofread for me, so she gave it to Anna. She showed her the section titled "Show How to Pretend" and told her to do some of these things with the kids. They had fun for hours combining "Play with Stuffed Animals" and "Roll Playing" activities.

Playing with trucks and cars

They already know how to race and crash!

- going on a trip
- delivering things
- creating a little city using blocks, boxes, sand, etc.

Play with dolls or stuffed animals

- Make a zoo with the stuffed animals then have the dolls visit.
- Be a lifeguard, fireman, policeman, or superhero who protects and saves the action figures.
- Create a pretend family.
- Be a pilot, bus driver, train conductor, or captain of a ship - with stuffed animal passengers (perhaps their bed can be the vehicle, or you can build one from pillows).
- Have a tea party.
- Pretend they are doing all the things the child does each day (you can go through the whole day from waking up to getting tucked in).
- Have them put on a show (it can be a way to get a shy child singing – after all it's just the teddy bear singing the song).

Role Playing

Create a costume box to play make believe with dress-up costumes made from:

• ties	• briefcase or purse
• scarves	• hats
• towels	• bathrobe
• fabric	• your clothes

You can collect items from thrift stores, garage sales or your own closet – including props and accessories.

You can become:

- royalty
- pirates
- rock stars
- animals
- firefighters
- astronauts
- explorers

Role playing is also a great way to teach children how to act in different situations by pretending you are going places and doing things such as:

- a restaurant
- a kids party
- a formal tea party
- going to the store
- the library
- a museum
- going to school or church
- hiking in the woods
- the dentist or doctor
- a wedding
- going to the movies (you can take tickets, make popcorn, darken the room, and then watch a short video).

Playing with real things

Two year olds love their toys, but they also love to play with real things. Your house is full of perfectly safe items that a child can play with:

- A cardboard box – depending on the size – can become a jewelry box, treasure chest, car, boat, or a house . . . Get an appliance box from a store that sells stoves and refrigerators, cut a door and windows in it and give your preschooler crayons or markers to decorate their little house inside and out.
- Pots and pans and wooden spoons make fun drum sets, or for pretending to cook.
- Empty paper towel rolls can be used as musical instruments, a spyglass to look through, or for sword

fighting. And look for other potential toys in your recycle bin.

- Indoor water play: lay out a towel on the floor (wood, tile or vinyl – not carpeted) put a jellyroll pan, cookie sheet, or cutting board in the middle of the towel and give your child a variety of small plastic, metal, or wood cups, bowls, scoops and spoons - and a cup full of water.
- Blankets or sheets can turn chairs or a table into a playhouse, a cave, fort, or a tent.
- Pillows and blankets can become a nest or a boat.

Making Something Together

When you make something together you not only create something real, but you create a wonderful memory, and sometimes a keepsake that will remind the child of the time you spent together having fun. Here are some ideas:

- simple arts and crafts – where they can do most of the work themselves
- stringing beads to make bracelets (watch extra closely)
- find a roly-poly bug under a rock, put it in a jar, collect thing for it to climb on – and watch it together. Lady bugs and grasshoppers are great too, but harder to find.
- baking a cake, making cookies
- planting a garden or just a few beans in a jar
- picking flowers and putting them in a vase together (if you have a tiny vase you can search for flowers in the grass)
- taping artwork to the walls to create a little art gallery and post pictures of it on Facebook
- printing photos and making a real photo album

- making a Facebook photo album together
- making a collage of baby pictures of everyone in the family

Making a little photo album can create a special treasure. Many children don't really get to look at pictures of their family, relatives, and themselves – except for a quick look at the back of the digital camera right after you take it. Your photos are in the computer. It's easy to get some printed at the drug store, and buy a little photo album there too – the kind with one photo to a page. You can show your little one how to put the pictures into the plastic sleeve, as you talk together about the people in the pictures. They are so proud of themselves when they show it to someone, both for making it and for being able to name the people and talk about the pictures. They can take it with them if they are spending the night away from home, and you might just find your little one quietly looking through it.

For some children, drawing or painting can become a time to "work on skills" more than a time for creating art work.

> I was visiting my daughter Heather when her two-year-old son had just become very interested in drawing circles. If we ever needed to change his activity all we had to do was invite him to sit in his highchair and color. He made page after page of little and big circles and spirals. Outside he would use sidewalk chalk to draw circles everywhere. One day, when he was coloring, I sat beside him and drew pictures too. I didn't say, "I'm going to teach you to draw faces." An older child would love to hear that, but Carsten had just turned two so I just started to slowly draw, as he watched. First I carefully made a circle like the ones he was doing, then I added a curved line and two tiny circles, and suddenly the circle had become a happy-face! He watched spellbound as I drew a few more. After that he began adding random lines and tiny circles to his pictures. A couple weeks after I returned home Heather emailed me pictures of Carsten's latest drawings: pages filled with colorful happy-faces!

Made-up Games

Sarah made up a game. Little Joseph learned nursery rhymes and little poems as she read them over and over. Then they play Say The Missing Word: "Hickory, dickory, _____. The mouse ran up the _____." He loves it. And he's so proud of himself! Once it's really easy for him, she makes it a little harder – until he is saying almost every other word.

They also make up stories. Joseph holds his hand like a little open book then has Mom start reading, leaving out words for Joseph to fill in to make the story his own. For example,

Mom: "One day Joseph looked out the window and saw _____."
Joseph: "A fire truck!"
Mom: "The fire truck was _____"
Two-year-old Joseph actually invented this game!

Charity and Marian (Mimi) play "Magic Rocket Ship." Mimi gets under a blanket, they count down, make rocket sounds, and then when they land Mimi opens the rocket door (throws off the blanket) and Charity says "Wow, we've landed at _____ !" then Mimi announces the destination and off they go around the house playing visiting the children's museum or the zoo . . .

I like to play Changing from Caterpillar to Butterfly with my grandkids. After crawling around being a hungry caterpillar my grandchild wraps up in a blanket (taking a large colorful scarf) then pops out as a butterfly dancing and running around with fluttering silk wings!

When I was little we played games that even a two year old might enjoy. Try having the child leave the room and then hide a small object in plain sight – and see if they can find it. It's kind of like Where's Waldo – harder than it sounds - you have to give hints – "you're getting warmer."

You might remember games you played as a child that are simple enough to teach a preschooler. You can make up new games of your own. Get ideas for games on the internet. Follow your child's lead and make up a new game together. Or just play traditional games like hide and seek.

Preschoolers love singing motion songs – like The Wheels on the Bus, learning sign language, dancing, and action nursery rhymes like "This is the Way the Ladies Ride" and "This Little Piggy Went to Market."

Do your exercise workout with them. Put on music and do aerobics – or just dance!

Playing Outdoors

Have you ever heard or said "use your indoor voice," or "don't run in the house?" There is great freedom in playing outdoors. There are things you can do outside that may not be allowed inside like:

- jump
- yell
- throw and kick a ball
- run around
- play with sand, water, leaves
- blow bubbles
- learn how to roll down hill

Kids need to do things like these! They need to be in a variety of environments for their proper development. They need to run around on sloping and uneven ground, not just perfectly flat floors. They need to be in open areas where they can see things that are a mile away, not just flat walls fifteen feet away.

The outdoors has so many interesting shapes, surfaces, and sizes for them to see and touch. Investigate the rough tree bark, hard rock, shapes of leaves and colors of flowers. Teach them to wonder at clouds, sunsets, tall trees, flying birds, the wind, and the moon. Children don't always notice these things automatically. Once when my daughters were children I pointed out a rainbow when a friend was with them. She was about ten years old and she said it was the first rainbow she had ever seen. I was shocked – how sad. Imagine all the rainbows she missed just because she wasn't looking for them.

Water!

There are so many ways kids can play with water outside on a warm day. Some possibilities are:

- a dish pan full of water and cups, a funnel, and bowls; toy boats; help them find things that float or sink; wash rocks or anything washable
- empty shampoo bottle full of water to squirt
- a spray bottle full of water
- a big paint brush and bucket of water to paint the concrete, fence, walls, rocks...
- water the plants
- make mud pies
- learn to pour water from plastic bottles to cups
- squirt guns
- the hose, sprinkler, or a shallow wading pool

Once again, remember:

The more water the more closely you watch.

Games

Many games that you can only play outside:

- shadow tag – trying to step on the other person's shadow without letting them step on yours
- any other game of tag (like "freeze-tag")
- catch (start with rolling the ball)
- races – running, hopping, rolling . . .
- ring-around-the-rosy, London bridge (to two and three year olds nothing is corny or uncool)

Clearly exercise is good for all of us and really important for children's developing bodies. But there are also some immediate benefits from letting little ones play outside. After all that free play and exercise they will:

- be calmer indoors
- sleep so much better at night.

As I noted before, the weather doesn't have to be perfect for outdoor play. Of course lightning and high winds are a safety issue, and extreme heat and cold, or wet (when it's cold), might be a health issue. In hot weather always give them plenty of water to drink. But I never let just the fact that "it's nicer in the air conditioning" be a reason to keep them inside all day.

If you don't have a yard, go to a park or just take a walk. Taking a walk together should be a special time to share. In my work I get to do a lot of people watching, (sitting around at art shows waiting to sell a painting) and more than once I've seen a little girl trying to show some delightful discovery to her mother who is talking on a cell phone, ignoring her completely. It breaks my heart.

So, when you are there – be there. Talk about what you see, or what you did yesterday. Search together for rocks one day, then notice every flower the next. Of course your child will want to have input, and you may end up spending weeks collecting leaves every time you step outside together – but that's okay. And if you must take a cell phone call, do just what you would do if you were with an important adult: ask to be excused for a moment, then keep the call short.

11.

Homeschooling With Preschoolers

It is a big challenge to be able to effectively teach the older children at home, when you have a preschooler. If you are planning to homeschool your children, and your first child is a young preschooler now, you will still have times when you need to get things done without all the interruptions. The good news is that it's important for children to learn to play quietly by themselves.

After age three you can give them more coloring books & pages and workbooks – that seem like "real" schoolwork. But there is no curriculum you can purchase that could ever teach a two, three, or four year old all the things they need to learn. Luckily the child comes

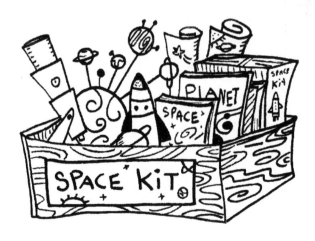

equipped with a built-in curriculum that will guide them in learning the vast amount of knowledge that needs to be absorbed during this stage of life.

Sitting the child down to tell them information will usually just take time away from their most valuable 'lessons.' Preschool age children need to learn: good behavior, self-control, language, basic life skills, how to do chores, singing, games, sports skills, artistic skills, information about nature and science, and everything else. They learn it best - not by being taught about it - but by doing it. They explore, experiment, practice, and imitate.

This book is about how you can help them with this. But your little one shouldn't be consuming your attention all the time. That's not healthy for either of you. Every preschooler needs to spend some time exploring, experimenting, practicing skills, and copying others, without constant assistance. If you homeschool older children, and have a preschooler – your little one can still be actively learning. Here are some ideas to make homeschooling with preschoolers in the house a lot easier. A Special Box of Toys and Treasures

One of the most effective ways to keep your preschooler or toddler engaged in play while you are teaching the older kids is to have a special box full of special toys that are only brought out while the other children are being homeschooled. There can be a random variety of different kinds of toys that can be safely played with without help from anyone. Some can be very simple — miniature baby dolls, little plastic animals, tea set, cars . . . a little different than the ones they can play with just any time. Novelty items like windup toys and bunny ears. Educational toys, like a wooden puzzle, kaleidoscope, or toy for practicing Velcro, buttons, zippers . . . maybe a purse or little box filled with special treasures.

Always announce that it is Learning Time and they get to play with their special box of toys now! Be sure to let them know when it is just about time to put it away, and give them warning in advance. Also have a new activity to move on to — like lunch or playing outside.

Include them in the Homeschooling

The toy and treasure box will only keep the child occupied for so long, so you can use the natural desire for your little one to do what the big kids are doing. You can have homeschool work that your little one can sit at a desk or table and do. Sticker books, and pads of blank paper to draw or color in, coloring books, and paint-with-water books are great because they will feel like they are doing real schoolwork. Put your preschooler's books and papers in the same kind of folders, files, school bags or stacks that you use for the older children. And put them away when Learning Time is over.

Your child may enjoy play dough (homemade or store bought), cutting and pasting to create a collage, looking at books, or ideas you find in the Chapter 9, Fun-School Activities. Anything the child can do sitting at a table that doesn't require much assistance.

One of my homeschooling daughters has a set of little boxes labeled: "coloring time," "painting time," "reading time," "Lego time," and "play-dough time." In each box are all the supplies you need for each activity. The reading time box is filled with little board books and mini books like DK Pocket Genius books. These are kept out of reach and out of sight. They come down during homeschool time, or when there is a babysitter.

Nap Time

You can include a nap in your preschooler's schedule and plan important discussion and teaching during their naptime. At daycare centers (and in many homes), every child four, or even five, years old and younger takes a daily nap at the same time every day.

If you think this will fit into your family's lifestyle and decide to try it, have a regular schedule of calming activities that lead up to naptime. Be firm and don't give in and don't give up.

Be like Mary Poppins - someone they just can't win a fight with. It may take some time before the child starts to feel sleepy at naptime, but just stick with it.

Add Childcare to the Older Children's Curriculum

If you have a large family you can schedule each of the older children to watch the toddler for a half hour or an hour, while you teach the other children their individual lessons. Use it as a time for learning valuable parenting and childcare skills by having them do activities described in this book.

Give the older child lots of direction; train them to care for the toddler. Make sure they really understand that they are helping with their little brother or sister's mental, social and physical development. And encourage them to have fun together!

You can even have them write a weekly report about their activities; research to find new ideas; plan a schedule of activities; or a teen could even create a babysitter's blog with great ideas and photos for babysitting.

Help Them Have Fun

Chances are you'll need to use several of these ideas each day – maybe even all of them! Just remember, a toddler who is having fun, will stay focused longer. So be encouraging, enthusiastic but calm, and set the tone for your little one.

Raising preschool age children is a lot of work. There is a reason public schools don't take them until they are five years old! Just being with them takes a commitment of time and energy, but that doesn't mean it can't be fun.

Two Year Olds

A two year old is a non-verbal thinker who is motivated by an irresistible drive to learn. They cannot think like us yet and they cannot deny their urge to study, discover, and teach themselves everything they need to know and do and to be in order to survive and thrive in their world.

My Notes:

Three Year Olds

Three year olds are becoming more social. Friends become more important to them. They love pretending to be someone important, asking question after question, and playing all kinds of games. They want to be like the big kids.

My Notes:

Four Year Olds

Four year olds are naturally curious, creative and confident. The parents' challenge is to keep increasing the level of difficulty and complexity in crafts, toys, and games to match their growing skills and interests, while answering, and helping the child to find answers to, all those question.

My Notes:

The Joy of Teaching at Home

Teaching two, three, and four year olds at home is just helping them to learn and develop so they are ready for the more structured and academic learning of kindergarten and first grade. But it can always be fun-schooling! You can judge a preschoolers readiness for phonics, reading, and math, by their interest and enjoyment of it. Generally, workbooks and drills are not only unnecessary, they would take time away from the most important lessons: experimenting with, building, creating, exploring, discovering, talking about, and listening to whatever interests them at that moment. That is where most of the real learning takes place.

Education isn't about learning particular information according to a certain schedule – especially for preschoolers! It's about discovering, understanding, and learning at the pace and in the way that is best for that individual child. There is nothing I know of that is more important to a good education than keeping the love of learning, curiosity, and creativity alive.

Understanding your little one today can help you establish a great relationship based on love and respect that will continue to bless their childhood – and your whole life together.

Resources and References

Chapter 2

1. J. Ronald Lally. *The Science and Psychology of Infant-toddler Care.* www.zerotothree.org. 2003. Is a great resource for more information on this topic.

2. Joan Beck. *How to Raise a Brighter Child.* Pocket Books. New York. 1999. Is a great resource for more information on this topic.

Chapter 5

3. Brock Eide, M.D., M.A., and Fernette Eide, M.D. *The Mislabeled Child.* Hyperion. New York. 2006. (p172)

4. The Mislabeled Child. The authors explain that children will learn more easily and do better in school if the adults in their lives have been speaking with them in clear rich language. Babies and young children love to listen. Their little brains are busy filing away words, fitting together the structure of the language.

Chapter 7

5. Gayle Erwin. http://www.servant.org/

Chapter 9

8. MaLesa Breeding. Dana Hood. Jerry Whitworth. *Let All the Children Come to Me.* Cook Communications Ministries. Colorado Springs, CO. 2006. (Page 108)

Chapter 10

9. Jill Stamm, Ph.D. *Bright from the Start.* Gotham books. New York. 2007.

30322834R00064

Made in the USA
Middletown, DE
21 March 2016